MACBETH

by
William Shakespeare

Student Packet
Written by
Mary L. Dennis
Maureen Kirchhoefer, M.A.

Contains masters for:

- 1 Anticipation Guide
- 5 Vocabulary Activities
- 1 Study Guide
- 2 Critical Thinking Activities
- 2 Creative Writing Activities
- 7 Literary Analysis Activities
- 1 Review Activity
- 4 Comprehension Quizzes
- 2 Unit Exams (Objective and Essay)

PLUS Detailed Answer Key

Note
The text used to prepare this guide was the softcover Pelican Shakespeare published by The Penguin Group, edited by Alfred Harbage, ©1956, 1971 by Penguin Books; 1984 by Viking Penguin. The page references may differ in the hardcover or other paperback editions.

Please note: Please assess the appropriateness of this book for the age level and maturity of your students prior to reading and discussing it with your class.

ISBN 1-56137-437-7

Copyright infringement is a violation of Federal Law.

© 2000 by Novel Units, Inc., Bulverde, Texas. All rights reserved. No part of this publication may be reproduced, translated, stored in a retrieval system, or transmitted in any way or by any means (electronic, mechanical, photocopying, recording, or otherwise) without prior written permission from Novel Units, Inc.

Photocopying of student worksheets by a classroom teacher at a non-profit school who has purchased this publication for his/her own class is permissible. Reproduction of any part of this publication for an entire school or for a school system, by for-profit institutions and tutoring centers, or for commercial sale is strictly prohibited.

Novel Units is a registered trademark of Novel Units, Inc. Printed in the United States of America.

To order, contact your local school supply store, or—
Novel Units, Inc.
P.O. Box 97
Bulverde, TX 78163-0097

Web site: www.educyberstor.com

Name_____

Macbeth
Activity #1: Anticipation Guide
Use Before Reading

Anticipation Guide

Discuss the statements below with a small group. Write "A" next to statements with which your group agrees. If you disagree with the statement, write "D." If your group can not come to consensus, write "NC."

_____ 1. People who are striving to get ahead often step on other people.

_____ 2. You shouldn't put too much faith in fortune-tellers and others who claim to be able to predict the future.

_____ 3. Being powerful usually is the same thing as being happy.

_____ 4. People who are involved in criminal activities can still feel love, fear, and concern for other people.

_____ 5. Everyone is capable of murder under the right circumstances.

_____ 6. If you commit a crime and don't get caught, it doesn't really matter because your guilt over what you have done will destroy you in the end.

_____ 7. In feudal times, power over a kingdom usually passed peacefully from father to son.

_____ 8. One mistake can often lead to another.

_____ 9. The forces of good and evil are always locked in a struggle and probably always will be.

_____ 10. Witches have always existed; they still do today.

Macbeth, the play you are preparing to read, is one of Shakespeare's famous tragedies. From what members of your group know about **tragedy** as a literary form, what are some things which you might expect to find in this play?

Name_____

Macbeth
Activity #2
Vocabulary: *Act I*

Shakespeare often uses words that **seem** familiar to you—but their Elizabethan meanings were different. Some of the words below fall into this category and some don't. If the word has a **different** meaning today, write your own definition in the middle column and Shakespeare's meaning in the other column. If the word has the **same** meaning NOW as it did THEN, just fill in the right-hand column.

WORD	Today's definition, if different from the meaning in the play:	Definition as used in the play:
heath		
broil		
posters		
fantastical		
addition		
missives		
round		
illness		
seat		
convince		

Name_____

Macbeth
Activity #3
Vocabulary: *Act II*

Shakespearean language is easier to understand if you "translate" the lines into your own way of thinking. For instance, Banquo says:
  "Restrain in me the cursèd thoughts that nature
   Gives way to in repose."
You might say, "I have been having the weirdest thoughts in my dreams—I sure hope I don't have any more."

Rephrase each of the quotes below.

"So I lose none
 In seeking to augment it, but still keep
 My bosom franchised and allegiance clear,
 I shall be counselled." *(Banquo, sc. i)*

_____
_____
_____
_____

"The bell invites me.
 Hear it not, Duncan, for it is a knell
 That summons thee to heaven, or to hell."
 (Macbeth, sc. i)

_____
_____
_____
_____

"Th' attempt, and not the deed,
 Confounds us." *(Lady Macbeth, sc. ii)*

_____
_____

"No, this my hand will rather
 The multitudinous seas incarnadine,
 Making the green one red."
 (Macbeth, sc. ii)

_____
_____
_____
_____

"Most sacrilegious murder hath broke ope
 The Lord's anointed temple and stole thence
 The life o' th' building!" *(Macduff, sc. iii)*

_____
_____
_____

"The wine of life is drawn, and the mere lees
 Is left this vault to brag of." *(Macbeth, sc. iii)*

_____
_____

Name_____

Macbeth
Activity # 4
Vocabulary: *Act III*

In each of the sentences below, substitute a word from the vocabulary box for the underlined word in the sentence.

verities	parricide	avouch	scorched
jocund	measure	nonpareil	gospelled
oracles	rebuked	vizards	avaunt

1. The witches had some <u>truths</u> to tell in your case. _____

2. They could just as well be <u>soothsayers</u> for me. _____

3. They refuse to confess their <u>murder of their father</u>. _____

4. She <u>disapproved of</u> my plans. _____

5. Are you so <u>faithful to religious tenets</u> that you can pray even for your enemies? _____

6. I could convince myself to <u>justify</u> my own actions. _____

7. We have only <u>slashed</u> the snake. _____

8. If you don't want anyone to suspect anything, you'll have to act very <u>jovial</u> tonight. _____

9. You must think of your faces as <u>masks</u> to hide your true feelings. _____

10. Pour us all a <u>shot</u> of brandy; we'll drink to all these good friends. _____

11. Were you the one who murdered Fleance? Then you are <u>one who has no equal</u>. _____

12. <u>Go away!</u> _____

Name_____

Macbeth
Activity #5
Vocabulary: *Act IV*

Write the word from the vocabulary box next to its definition. Remember, Shakespeare's meanings often differ from the ones most familiar to us.

brinded	entrails	cauldron	adder
slab	germains	bodements	sceptres
blood-boltered	pernicious	firstlings	coz
gin	homely	laudable	folly
unsanctified	birthdom	dolor	redress
affeered	impediments	foisons	portable
at a point	relation	nice	stamp

1. riches _____
2. commendable _____
3. large kettle _____
4. snake _____
5. cousin _____
6. foolishness _____
7. striped _____
8. trap _____
9. unholy _____
10. coin _____
11. seeds _____
12. birthplace _____
13. armed _____
14. report _____
15. sticky _____
16. intestines _____
17. prophecies _____
18. swords _____
19. matted with blood _____
20. evil _____
21. first impulses _____
22. plain _____
23. sorrow _____
24. remedy _____
25. confirmed by law _____
26. obstacles _____
27. bearable _____
28. precise _____

© Novel Units, Inc.   All rights reserved

Name_____

Macbeth
Activity #6
Vocabulary: *Act V*

All of the answers for the crossword come from Act V of the play. Only a few can be found in standard dictionaries. Complete the puzzle by reviewing Act V, paying special attention to the footnoted words.

Across

3. habit
5. relatives
7. fool
9. A worthy king could be called a _____ flower.
11. One who is able to be hurt is _____.
13. more
14. tolled

Down

1. flu
2. Lady Macbeth's _____ summoned the doctor.
4. incapable of being gashed
6. examine
8. reported
10. widespread starvation
12. A barber in Shakespeare's time might exclaim, "What a lovely _____ of hair!"

© Novel Units, Inc.

8

All rights reserved

Name_____

Macbeth
Activity #7
Study Questions

Study Questions

Act I

1. For whom are the witches waiting?

2. What is King Duncan's reaction to the news that Cawdor is a traitor? What will happen to his title?

3. How do the witches greet Macbeth?

4. What predictions do the witches make?

5. Do Macbeth and Banquo have the same reaction to Ross' news?

6. What kind of person is Duncan?

7. What announcement is made about Malcolm? What is Macbeth's reaction?

8. How did Lady Macbeth find out about the witches' prophecies?

9. What is Lady Macbeth's main concern about her husband?

10. Did you find it amusing that Lady Macbeth was so pleasant to Duncan? Why?

11. How willing is Macbeth to go along with Lady Macbeth's plans for him to attain the throne?

12. How does Lady Macbeth convince Macbeth to murder Duncan?

Name_____

Macbeth
Study Questions • page 2

Act II

13. What does Macbeth want to discuss with Banquo? What is Banquo's reply?

14. What horrifying vision appears to Macbeth?

15. Why didn't Lady Macbeth kill Duncan herself? Who did?

16. Right after the murder, how do Lady Macbeth and Macbeth act?

17. Who comes to the castle early the next morning?

18. Who discovers Duncan's body?

19. How do Lady Macbeth and Macbeth try to avoid suspicion?

20. Who are Malcolm and Donalbain? Where do they go?

21. Who will be king now?

Act III

22. What does Macbeth decide about Banquo?

23. What happens when the murderers meet Banquo and Fleance?

24. What "surprise guest" do the Macbeths have for dinner? What problems does he cause?

25. Who is Hecate? What is her significance?

26. Where has Macduff gone? Why?

Name_____

Macbeth
Study Questions • page 3

Act IV

27. Why is Macbeth so anxious to find the witches? Do you think he's making a mistake?

28. Describe the apparitions and their messages.

29. How does Macbeth decide to retaliate against Macduff?

30. What does Malcolm need in the way of assurance from Macduff?

31. How has the English king offered to help defeat Macbeth?

Act V

32. How has Lady Macbeth changed since she was first seen in the play? What habits has she developed?

33. Why are Macbeth's robes said to "hang loose about him"?

34. Why is Macbeth so sure nothing bad will happen to him?

35. What clues do the soldiers' activities give you that Macbeth may be wrong?

36. What finally happens to Lady Macbeth?

37. Why is Macbeth so confident Young Siward won't kill him?

38. What surprise does Macduff spring on Macbeth?

39. What does Macduff bring to Malcolm?

40. Who will now be king of Scotland?

Name_____

Macbeth
Activity #8
Critical Thinking: Use After Act I

Before making any big decision, it is usually wise to weigh the pros and cons. Macbeth had some trouble deciding if he wanted to go along with his wife's plans to murder Duncan. Imagine you are "inside Macbeth's head," and list the pros and cons of this very important decision. Cite lines from the play as well as relating your own ideas about what you imagine Macbeth thought.

Pro	Con
"Yes, I think the best idea is to kill Duncan—tonight!"	"Kill Duncan? You must be out of your mind!"

Name_____

Macbeth
Activity #9
Creative Writing • Use After Act I

Lady Macbeth learned of the witches' predictions from a letter she received from her husband. He arrived home before she could write a reply, but suppose he had been delayed and Lady Macbeth had sent a letter back to him. Write her response below.

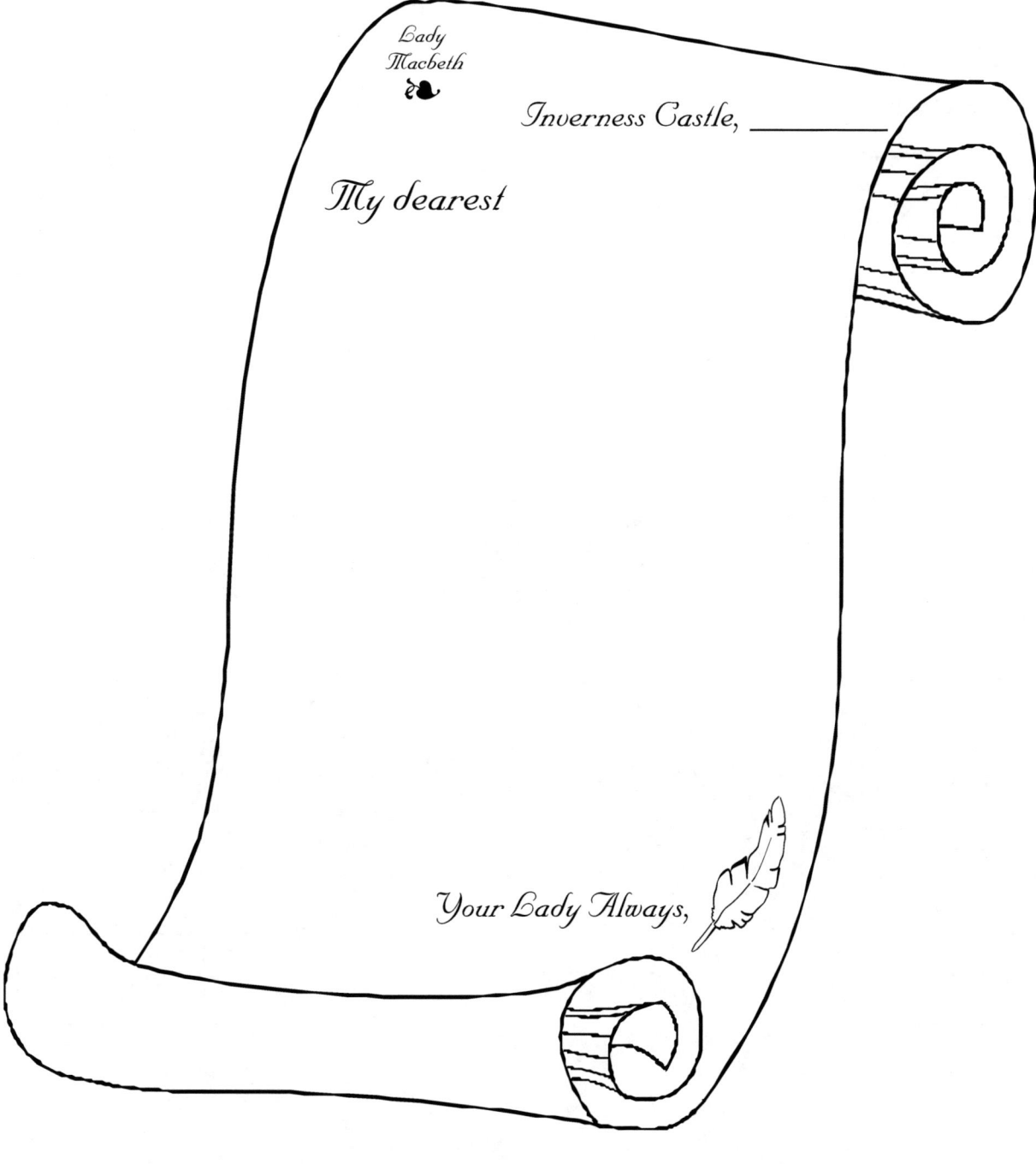

© Novel Units, Inc.   All rights reserved

Name_____

Macbeth
Activity #10: Character Analysis
Use After Act II

This sociogram can be used to summarize Macbeth's actions and feelings regarding other characters, and theirs toward him. Write words and phrases on the appropriate arrows.

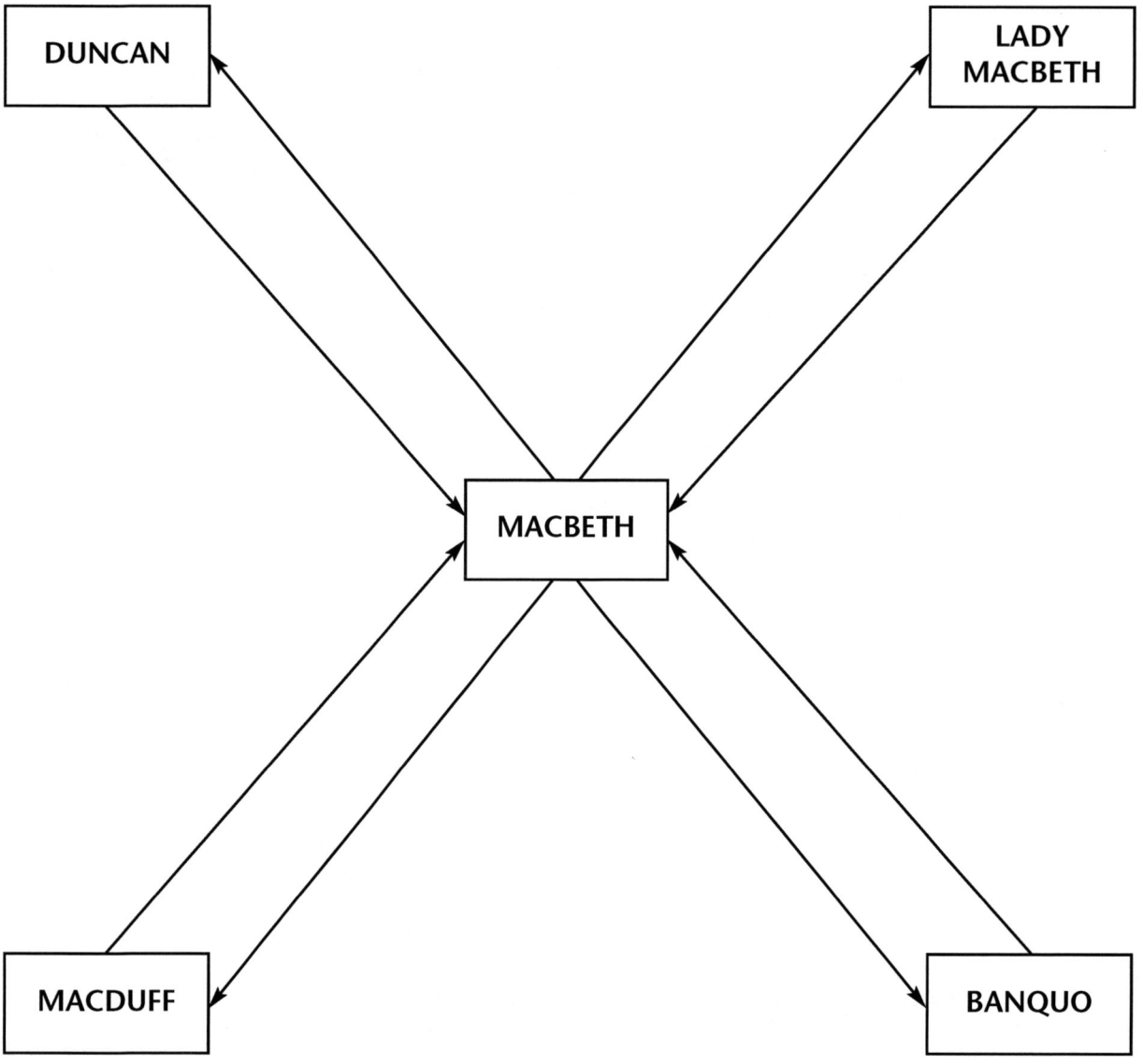

Name_____

Macbeth
Activity #11: Shakespeare's Meter
Use After Act II

Meter is the natural rhythm of language as it is spoken. The many different forms of meter are distinguished by the number of stressed and unstressed syllables in a line. The form most often used by Shakespeare was **iambic pentameter**. In this form, there are FIVE *(penta)* pairs of unstressed/stressed IAMBIC FEET to a line.

Example:

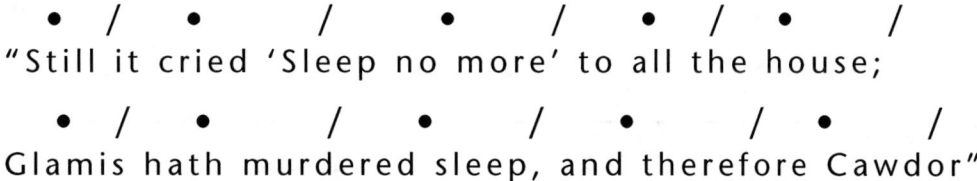

"Still it cried 'Sleep no more' to all the house;
Glamis hath murdered sleep, and therefore Cawdor"

Each • / is an iambic foot, and the process of marking the lines, as above, is called **scanning**. **Scan** the following lines by marking them like the example.

1. "Who was it that thus cried? Why, worthy Thane,

   You do unbend your noble strength to think

   So brainsickly of things. Go get some water

   And wash this filthy witness from your hand."

2. Now write your own lines of **iambic pentameter**:

_____
_____
_____
_____
_____
_____
_____
_____
_____
_____
_____
_____

Name_____

Macbeth
Activity #12: Antithesis
Begin after Act III

An **antithesis** is a situation in which the author places two sharply contrasting ideas side-by-side in parallel words, phrases, or structure. *Macbeth* begins with antithesis when the witches refer to the battle "lost and won" and conclude Act I, scene i, with "Fair is foul, and foul is fair." Skim the first three acts of the play to find other examples of antithesis. Then, as you finish reading add more examples. (Include Act, scene, line number, and speaker for each example you find.)

1. _____
   _____
   _____

2. _____
   _____
   _____

3. _____
   _____
   _____

4. _____
   _____
   _____

5. _____
   _____
   _____

6. _____
   _____
   _____

© Novel Units, Inc.   All rights reserved

Name_____

Macbeth
Activity #13: Author's Style
Use After Act III

Shakespeare used many **similes** and **metaphors** in his writing. A **simile** uses the words "like" or "as" to compare objects or ideas, while a **metaphor** is a more direct comparison of objects or ideas, and sometimes uses the word "is."

"…*as* two spent swimmers that do cling together and choke their art." (simile)
"That swiftest wing of recompense *is* slow to overtake thee." (metaphor)

Identify each quotation below as a metaphor or simile. Also indicate what is being compared. (Quotes are from the first three acts.)

Quotation	S=simile M=metaphor	What is being compared?
1. "New honors come upon him. Like our strange garments, cleave not to their mould but with the aid of use."		
2. "If you can look into the seeds of time and say which grain will grow and which will not…"		
3. "But signs of nobleness, like stars, shall shine on all deservers."		
4. "It was the owl that shrieked, the fatal bellman which gives the stern'st good-night."		
5. "Sleep that knits up the raveled sleave of care, the death of each day's life, sore labor's bath…"		
6. "Then comes my fit again. I had else been perfect; whole as the marble, founded as the rock, as broad and general as the casing air."		

Name_____

Macbeth
Activity #14: Character Analysis
Use After Act IV

At the beginning of the play, Macbeth was a courageous, loyal man with the respect and friendship of many. His encounter with the witches, however, began a series of changes in his personality. On the shield, write words and phrases that describe Macbeth at the beginning of the play. In the cauldron, write words that describe Macbeth now.

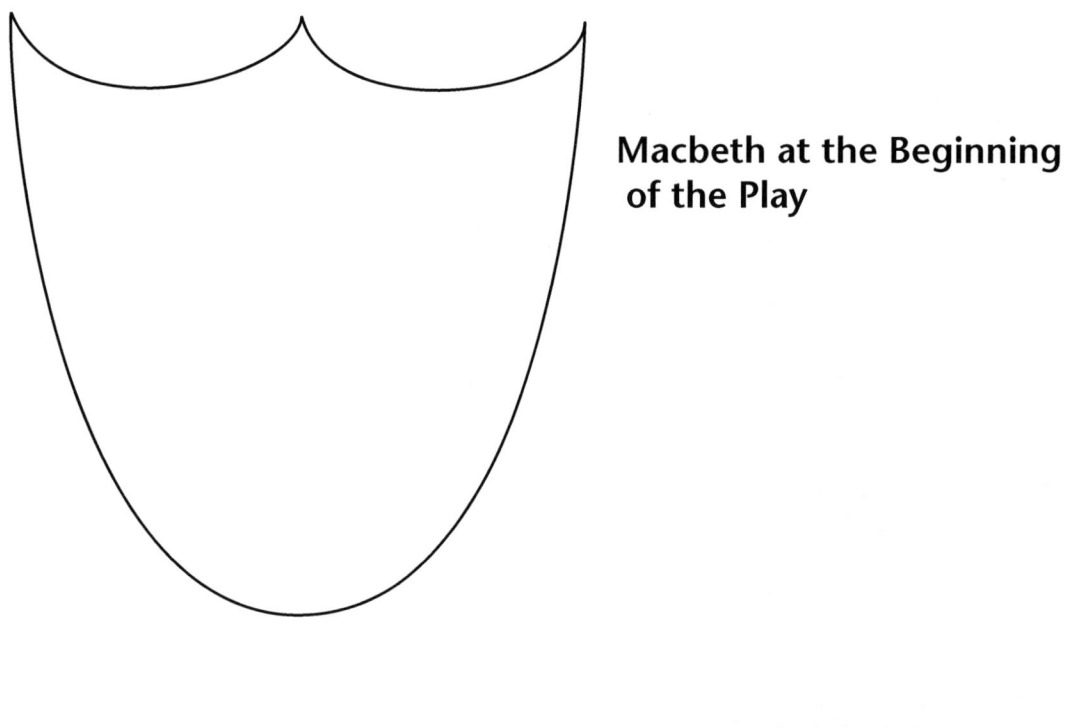

Macbeth at the Beginning of the Play

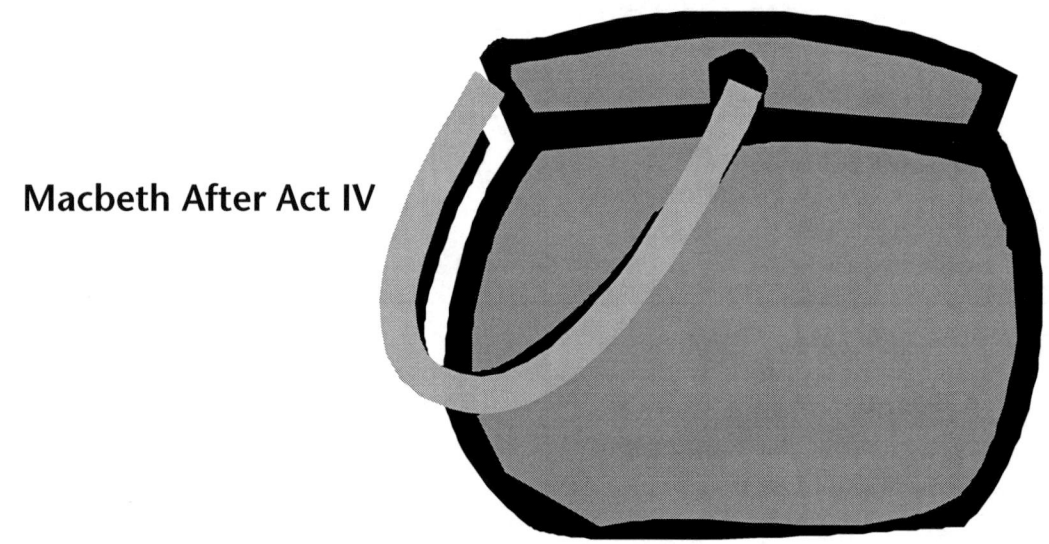

Macbeth After Act IV

Name_____

Macbeth
Activity #15: Values Study
Use After Reading

Place the names of each of the following characters on each of the scales, below. When you are finished, compare and contrast your answers with a partner's.

Macbeth   **Lady Macbeth**   **Banquo**   **Macduff**   **Duncan**

Gullible |—|—|—|—|—|—|— | Wary
                   0

Loyal |—|—|—|—|—|—|— | Disloyal
                   0

Concerned about Scotland |—|—|—|—|—|—|— | Concerned about Self
                   0

Not Jealous |—|—|—|—|—|—|— | Jealous
                   0

Clear-Thinking |—|—|—|—|—|—|— | Confused
                   0

Ambitious |—|—|—|—|—|—|— | Unambitious
                   0

© Novel Units, Inc.   All rights reserved

Name_____

Macbeth
Activity #16: Creative Writing
Use After Reading

| EXCLUSIVE! | *Kingdom Chronicle* | Today's Weather: |

June 10, 1040

Surprise Attack Ousts Macbeth

_____
_____
_____
_____
_____
_____
_____
_____
_____
_____
_____
_____

Today's Reader Survey:
_____
_____
_____ ?

Drop off your YES or NO answer by tomorrow at
_____
_____

Obituaries

Lady Macbeth_____
_____
_____
_____
_____
_____

Macbeth_____
_____
_____
_____
_____

Young Siward_____
_____
_____
_____
_____

Add your own pages with articles, cartoons, ads, etc.

Doctor, Gentlewoman Relate Strange Incidents at Dunsinane

_____
_____
_____
_____
_____
_____
_____

Name_____

Macbeth
Activity #17: Character Analysis
Use After Reading

You're the Director!

When a casting director chooses actors and actresses for a play or film, he or she must worry first about the LEADING ROLES, then the SUPPORTING ROLES, then the MINOR CHARACTERS, who have names but don't say much or have large parts, and finally the EXTRAS, who don't have names and may not even speak (for instance, people in the background in a scene which takes place in public).

Use the target below to categorize the characters needed for a film version of *Macbeth*. Put the leading characters in the middle and work your way out, with the extras in the outer circle.

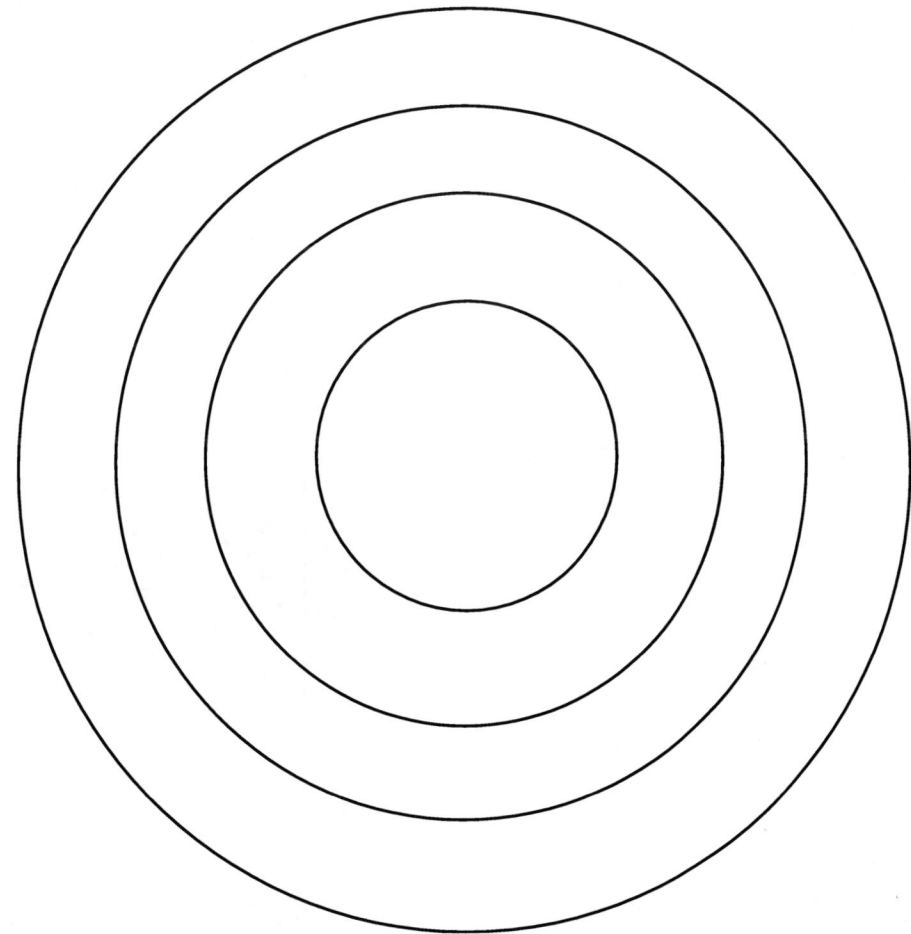

Name_____

Macbeth
Activity #18: Review/Critical Thinking/Cooperative Activity
Use After Reading

Properties

Items used in the play, other than scenery and costumes, are called **properties** or "props." The Prop Manager is in charge of determining the props needed for a production of a play, locating the props, and making sure they are all on hand before a performance. Your group is responsible for listing the props needed for one act of *Macbeth.* You should also list one or more places where you will probably be able to locate the props listed.

Act # _____

Prop Needed:	For: (Character)	Find at:

© Novel Units, Inc.   All rights reserved

Name_____

Macbeth
Activity #19: Review/Cooperative Activity
Use After Reading

As your group reviews the events and characters in the play, use the chart below as a guide and jot down your own notes for review before testing.

Macbeth	Lady Macbeth	The Witches	Macduff
Setting	Conflicts	Solutions	What was Shakespeare saying about ambition?
Values of Various Characters	Examples of Figurative Language	Good Parts for Oral Reading	Most Exciting Parts

Additional Notes: (Use back of paper.)

Name_____

Macbeth
Vocabulary Quiz
Use After Reading

Part One.
Directions: Shakespeare's meanings are often not the same as ours. For each word, choose the <u>Shakespearean</u> meaning.

1. broil   A. cooking method   B. battle   C. involve
2. posters   A. swift travelers   B. equestrians   C. large pictures
3. fantastical   A. wonderful   B. unlikely   C. imaginary
4. addition   A. extra room   B. title   C. math process
5. seat   A. chair   B. site   C. main town
6. guise   A. mask   B. secret   C. habit
7. patch   A. mend   B. fool   C. garden
8. cast   A. players   B. examine   C. remedy
9. fell   A. tripped   B. autumn   C. head
10. moe   A. comedian   B. more   C. nickname

Part Two.
Directions:
The quotes on the right have been rephrased. Choose the correct "translation" for each.

_____ 11. "So I lose none/ in seeking to augment it, but still keep My bosom franchised and allegiance clear,/ I shall be counselled."

_____ 12. "Th' attempt, and not the deed,/ Confounds us."

_____ 13. "Most sacrilegious murder hath broke ope/ The Lord's anointed temple and stole thence/ The life o' th' building!"

A. It is the fear of being caught, not the actual murder, that worries us.

B. As long as it involves no wrongdoing, I'm willing to talk with you about it.

C. Duncan is dead.

© Novel Units, Inc.   All rights reserved

Name_____

Macbeth
Vocabulary Quiz • page 2

Part Three.
Directions: The quotes below can be completed with words from the box. Indicate the letter of the correct word for each blank.

a. avouch
b. oracles
c. laudable
d. firstlings

e. verities
f. parricide
g. scorched

h. nonpareil
i. relation
j. vizards

k. jocund
l. folly
m. nice

_____ 14. "O, _____/
_____ 15. Too _____ and yet too true!"

_____ 16. "…to do harm/ Is often _____, to do good sometime/ Accounted
_____ 17. dangerous _____."

_____ 18. "The very _____of my heart shall be the _____ of my hand."

_____ 19. "Why by the _____on thee made good.
_____ 20. My they not be my _____ as well."

_____ 21. "In England and in Ireland, not confessing/ Their cruel _____…"

_____ 22. "…and though I could/ With barefaced power sweep him from my sight
         And bid my will _____ it, yet I must not,…"

_____ 23. "We have _____ the snake, not killed it."

_____ 24. "There's comfort yet; they are assailable.
         Then be thou _____."

_____ 25. "And make our faces _____ to our hearts
         Disguising what they are."

_____ 26. "Yet he's good that did the like for Fleance:
         If thou didst it, thou art the _____."

Name_____

Macbeth
Vocabulary Quiz • page 3

Part Four.
Directions: Match the definitions in the right-hand column to the vocabulary words in the box. Remember that Shakespeare's definitions often differ from ours.

a. snake	e. striped	i. sorrow	m. unholy
b. intestines	f. redden	j. dregs	n. riches
c. evil	g. seeds	k. coin	
d. open place	h. obstacles	l. trap	

_____ 27. brinded

_____ 28. gin

_____ 29. unsanctified

_____ 30. entrails

_____ 31. dolor

_____ 32. foisons

_____ 33. adder

_____ 34. stamp

_____ 35. germains

_____ 36. incarnadine

_____ 37. lees

_____ 38. pernicious

_____ 39. impediments

_____ 40. heath

© Novel Units, Inc.   All rights reserved

Name_____

Macbeth
ACT ONE QUIZ

Multiple Choice. Choose the BEST answer.

1. The battle described at the opening of the play was between Scotland and
   A. England   B. Norway   C. France   D. Ireland

2. Before we see Macbeth, we learn that he is a
   A. brave fighter   B. nobleman   C. king   D. A and B

3. The witches hailed Macbeth by all of these except
   A. Thane of Cawdor   C. King of Scotland
   B. Thane of Glamis   D. Duke of York

4. The witches prophesied that Banquo would be
   A. Thane of Cawdor   C. conqueror of England
   B. General of the king's army   D. the father of kings

5. Duncan named as his heir
   A. Macbeth   B. Banquo   C. Malcolm   D. Donalbain

6. Lady Macbeth learned of the witches' predictions from
   A. a letter   B. a messenger   C. Angus   D. Ross

7. Lady Macbeth eagerly welcomed Duncan to the castle because
   A. she was very fond of him
   B. she knew he would give her a handsome present
   C. she thought she could warn him about Macbeth
   D. she thought it would provide the opportunity needed to kill him

8. Macbeth hesitated to murder Duncan because
   A. he feared his wife would find out
   B. he thought Duncan's sons would kill him
   C. he really liked Duncan
   D. he wasn't sure the people would accept him as king

9. The person chiefly responsible for planning Duncan's murder was
   A. Macbeth   B. Lady Macbeth   C. Banquo   D. Malcolm

10. _____ will be blamed for Duncan's murder.
    A. Banquo   B. Donalbain   C. the grooms   D. Ross

© Novel Units, Inc.   All rights reserved

Name_____

Macbeth
ACT TWO QUIZ

Multiple Choice. Choose the BEST answer.

1. Just before the murder, Macbeth had a vision of a
   A. bell   B. light   C. dagger   D. crown

2. Lady Macbeth would have killed Duncan herself except
   A. she had no dagger   C. Macbeth did it first
   B. Duncan resembled her father   D. the sight of blood made her faint

3. Macbeth thought he heard _____ while he was murdering Duncan.
   A. footsteps   B. voices   C. knocking   D. a bell

4. Macbeth refused to smear the grooms with blood because
   A. he was feeling sick to his stomach.
   B. he was sure no one would believe they were guilty anyway.
   C. it had been agreed that Lady Macbeth would do it.
   D. he was afraid to return to the scene of the murder.

5. The steady knocking on the castle door was done by
   A. the porter   B. Macbeth   C. Macduff and Lennox   D. Malcolm

6. Duncan's body was discovered by
   A. Lennox   B. the porter   C. the grooms   D. Macduff

7. The grooms were killed by
   A. a servant   B. Macduff   C. Macbeth   D. suicide

8. When Lady Macbeth "learned" of the deaths in the castle, she
   A. displayed remarkable self-control.   C. glowed with satisfaction.
   B. flew into a rage.   D. pretended to feel faint.

9. Malcolm and Donalbain decided to flee Scotland because
   A. they had committed a crime.   C. they feared for their lives.
   B. Macduff suspected them.   D. they had no ambition.

10. Malcolm decided to go to
    A. England   B. Ireland   C. France   D. Norway

Name_____

Macbeth
ACT THREE QUIZ

Matching. Match the characters and actions. Some are used more than once.

_____ 1. killed by hired murderers
_____ 2. dismissed guests from the banquet
_____ 3. escaped from his father's killers
_____ 4. "surprise guest" seen only by Macbeth
_____ 5. had "a fit" at the feast
_____ 6. became angry with the three witches
_____ 7. disgraced by his failure to attend the feast
_____ 8. hired murderers to kill his friend
_____ 9. tries to calm down Macbeth and assures him he's being silly
_____ 10. hopeful Macduff can reclaim Scotland

A. Lady Macbeth
B. Macbeth
C. Banquo
D. Hecate
E. Macduff
F. Fleance
G. Lennox

True-False. Write "True" or "False" on the line before each statement.

_____ 11. Macbeth was bothered by the witches' prediction that Banquo would father kings.
_____ 12. The courtiers played a practical joke on Macbeth at the feast.
_____ 13. A lord reported to Lennox that Macduff fled to Ireland.
_____ 14. Lady Macbeth apologized to her husband's guests, explaining he had a headache.
_____ 15. Macbeth's "vision" at the feast was due to moonlight coming through the window.
_____ 16. Banquo had no hesitation about revealing his plans for the day to Macbeth.
_____ 17. Macbeth has been having a great deal of trouble sleeping.
_____ 18. Macbeth couldn't find an empty seat at the banquet table.
_____ 19. The queen of the witches helped them plan what will happen to Macbeth next.
_____ 20. Lennox suggests that Fleance killed his father, since the son fled after the death.

Name_____

Macbeth
ACT FOUR QUIZ

Short Answer. Write a brief but concise answer to each question.

1. Who says, "Double, double toil and trouble/Fire burn and cauldron bubble"?

   Describe the first three visions and their warnings.

   2.

   3.

   4.

5. Describe the fourth vision and its effect on Macbeth.

6. With whom does Macduff meet, and where?

7. Who does Macbeth have killed in this act?

8. Why did Malcolm tell Macduff that he (Malcolm) would be a worse tyrant than Macbeth?

9. Who brings Macduff the news about his family?

10. What does Macduff vow?

Name_____

Macbeth
OBJECTIVE UNIT EXAM

Multiple Choice. Choose the BEST answer for each question.

1. At the beginning of the play, Macbeth was
   A. Thane of Scotland
   B. Thane of Glamis
   C. Thane of Fife
   D. King of England

2. The setting of the play is mainly the country of
   A. Ireland   B. Scotland   C. Italy   D. England

3. Duncan named _____ as his successor to the throne.
   A. Malcolm   B. Macbeth   C. Ross   D. Fleance

4. The witches told Macbeth that he would be
   A. King
   B. The father of kings
   C. Thane of Cawdor
   D. Both A and C

5. The witches told Banquo
   A. he would be king
   B. he would be killed
   C. his descendants would be kings
   D. that he should be careful

6. Macbeth hired murderers to kill
   A. Malcolm   B. Duncan   C. Banquo   D. all of these

7. Lady Macbeth encouraged her husband to
   A. kill Macduff
   B. kill Duncan
   C. leave Scotland
   D. give up the throne

8. At the banquet, what upset Macbeth and eventually resulted in the guests begin asked to leave?
   A. the appearance of Banquo's ghost
   B. the poisoning of the food
   C. the vision of the dagger
   D. Lady Macbeth's hand-washing complex

9. As Macbeth and Lady Macbeth destroyed the lives of others
   A. they became more and more content with their own lives
   B. Macbeth weakened and Lady Macbeth became more greedy
   C. their own lives became more and more unpleasant
   D. they rejoiced in their growing power

Name_____

Macbeth
OBJECTIVE UNIT EXAM
page 2

10. After he visited the witches the second time, why did Macbeth feel safe?
    A. "None of woman born shall harm Macbeth."
    B. "Macbeth shall live the least of nature."
    C. "Macbeth shall never vanquished be/ Until Great Birnam Wood to high Dunsinane Hill shall come against him."
    D. Both B and C
    E. Both A and C

11. What cruel action did Macbeth order to insure his status?
    A. the death of Malcolm
    B. the deaths of Macduff's wife and children
    C. the death of Donalbain
    D. all of these

12. Who committed suicide after loss of spirit and sanity?
    A. Lady Macbeth   C. Macbeth
    B. Lady Macduff   D. Macduff

13. The turning point of *Macbeth* is when
    A. Macbeth meets with the witches the second time.
    B. Lennox tells Macbeth that Macduff has left the country.
    C. the woods begin to move.
    D. the ghost of Banquo appears.

14. The <u>main</u> theme of *Macbeth* is
    A. It's best not to consort with witches.
    B. A person should remain loyal to his or her king.
    C. It is impossible to fight against Fate.
    D. Unrestrained ambition has devastating effects.

15. "Life's but a walking shadow, a poor player
    That struts and frets his hour upon the stage
    And then is heard no more."   These lines reflect Macbeth's
    A. realization that life is fruitless and futile
    B. sorrow over the death of Macduff
    C. regret that he is about to die
    D. atonement for his sins

Name_____

Macbeth
OBJECTIVE UNIT EXAM
page 3

Matching. For each group, match the character with the correct description.

_____ 16. Banquo   A. thinks he sees a knife before his eyes
_____ 17. Macduff   B. told his sons would be kings
_____ 18. Macbeth   C. rewards Macbeth with title of Thane of Cawdor
_____ 19. Duncan   D. a nobleman
_____ 20. Lennox   E. discovers Duncan has been murdered

_____ 21. Lady Macbeth   A. son of Duncan
_____ 22. Malcolm   B. predict Macbeth's future
_____ 23. Ross   C. reports Macbeth's success in battle
_____ 24. Fleance   D. is the planner of Duncan's murder
_____ 25. three witches   E. escapes from the murderers

Significant Passages
The purpose of this section is to show that you can interpret passages correctly, considering both the situation in which the passage occurs and the peculiarities of Elizabethan language. For each passage, the speaker and location in the play are given to help you place the situation in your mind. Choose the letter of the best interpretation.

_____ 26. "Fair is foul and foul is fair:
          Hover through the fog and filthy air." (The Witches, Act I, sc. i)
The witches

   A. go out only in bad weather.
   B. are clever at telling the difference between right and wrong.
   C. cause moral standards to be completely reversed.

_____ 27. "Dismayed not this
          Our captains, Macbeth and Banquo?"
          "Yes;
          As sparrows eagles, or the hare the lion." (Duncan, Captain, Act I, sc. ii)
The captain meant that

   A. Macbeth and Banquo were greatly disturbed by the assault
   B. the assault disturbed them no more than a hare would a lion
      or a sparrow would an eagle
   C. Macbeth and Banquo fought desperately

Name_____

Macbeth
OBJECTIVE UNIT EXAM
page 4

_____ 28. "He hath honored me of late, and I have bought
Golden opinions from all sorts of people,
Which would be worn now in their newest gloss,
Not cast aside so soon." (Macbeth, Act I, sc. vii)

Macbeth meant

A. He wanted to continue enjoying the honor and esteem he had honestly won.
B. He didn't want to cast aside all the people he had bribed until he got all he could from them.
C. People's good opinions of him were meaningless next to the honor bestowed by the king.

_____ 29. "Thou marshall'st me the way that I was going;
And such an instrument I was to use." (Macbeth, Act II, sc. i)

Macbeth meant

A. You urge me to the action I was planning, suggesting the same instrument that I had in mind.
B. You will have to lead me to Duncan's room; it is so dark I can't see.
C. My eyes can't fool me into thinking there is a dagger leading me to Duncan.

_____ 30. "Where we are,
There's daggers in men's smiles; the near in blood,
The nearer bloody." (Donalbain, Act II, sc. iii)

Donalbain meant

A. We must look pleasant and smile though in our hearts we feel quite the opposite.
B. We can't trust the smiles of those around us; those related to us are the most likely to be murderers.
C. We mustn't smile or someone will think we murdered our father.

_____ 31. "Naught's had, all's spent,
Where our desire is got without content.
'Tis safer to be that which we destroy
Than by destruction dwell in doubtful joy." (Lady Macbeth, Act III, sc. ii)

Lady Macbeth meant

A. After you spend all your money, there's nothing left but worry.
B. Getting what you want is not always worth the pain that follows.
C. It is best to destroy what stands in one's way.

© Novel Units, Inc.   All rights reserved

Name_____

Macbeth
OBJECTIVE UNIT EXAM
page 5

_____ 32. "There's blood upon thy face."
"'Tis Banquo's then."
" 'Tis better thee without than he within."
(Macbeth, Murderer, Act III, sc. iv)

Macbeth meant

    A. I'd rather have you outside the door than Banquo in this room.
    B. I'd rather have the blood on your face than still inside Banquo.
    C. I'd rather you hadn't come here with blood on your face.

_____ 33. "I am in blood
Stepped in so far that, should I wade no more,
Returning were as tedious as go o'er." (Macbeth, Act III, sc. iv)

Macbeth meant

    A. I have gotten so carried away with these crimes that I am disgusted with myself. I'm going to reform at once.
    B. As difficult as it will be to make restitution for what I have done, I intend to do it.
    C. I have gone so far with these crimes that it makes no difference now if I commit more.

_____ 34. "Out, damned spot! Out, I say! One—two—why then 'tis time to do't." (Lady Macbeth, Act V, sc. i)

These lines refer to

    A. a spot of blood that cannot be washed out of her gown.
    B. her guilt over the murders, which is driving her crazy.
    C. her amazement over the slaughtering of Macduff's family.

_____ 35. "And that which should should accompany old age
As honor, love, obedience, troops of friends,
I must not look to have; but in their stead,
Curses, not loud but deep, mouth honor, breath,
Which the poor heart would fain deny, and dare not."
(Macbeth, Act V, sc. iii)

Macbeth meant

    A. Taking the throne by murdering Duncan will not bring Macbeth the joys he would have had if he had attained his role honestly.
    B. People say the right things, but talk behind his back.
    C. Both A and B.

Name_____

Macbeth
OBJECTIVE UNIT EXAM
page 6

Quote Identification. Identify the speaker of each set of lines by choosing a character from the list on the right.

_____ 36. "Pray you keep seat.
The fit is momentary; upon a thought
He will again be well."

_____ 37. "Filthy hags! Why do you show me this?
...Now I see 'tis true;
For the blood-boltered Banquo
smiles upon me!..."

A. Duncan
B. Macbeth
C. Banquo
D. Doctor
E. Lady Macbeth
F. Macduff
G. Hecate

_____ 38. "Is execution done on Cawdor? Are not
Those in commission yet returned?"

_____ 39. "More needs she the divine than the physician."

_____ 40. "Yet do I fear thy nature.
It is too full o' th' milk of human kindness
To catch the nearest way."

_____ 41. "Is this a dagger which I see before me,
The handle toward my hand?"

_____ 42. "Well, may you see things well done there. Adieu,
Lest our old robes sit easier than our new!"

_____ 43. "O, treachery! Fly, good Fleance, fly, fly, fly!"

_____ 44. "Have I not reason, beldams as you are,
Saucy and overbold? How did you dare
To trade and traffic with Macbeth..."

_____ 45. "We will establish our estate upon
Our eldest, Malcolm, whom we name hereafter
The Prince of Cumberland."

Name_____

Macbeth
OBJECTIVE UNIT EXAM
page 7

Plot Map Matching. The quotes below the plot map correspond to points on the map. Match the event the quote brings to mind with its significance in the plot.

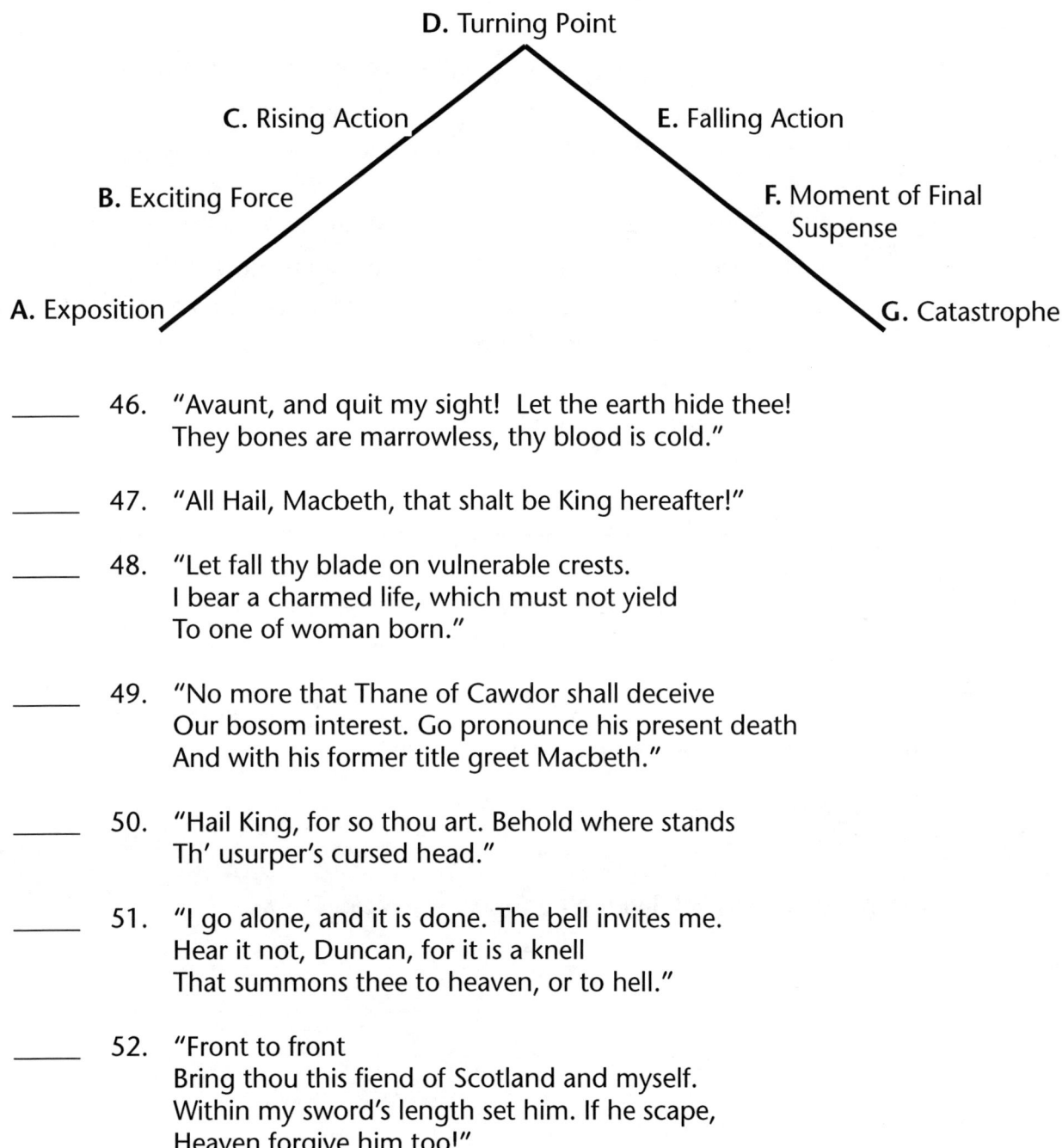

_____ 46. "Avaunt, and quit my sight! Let the earth hide thee!
They bones are marrowless, thy blood is cold."

_____ 47. "All Hail, Macbeth, that shalt be King hereafter!"

_____ 48. "Let fall thy blade on vulnerable crests.
I bear a charmed life, which must not yield
To one of woman born."

_____ 49. "No more that Thane of Cawdor shall deceive
Our bosom interest. Go pronounce his present death
And with his former title greet Macbeth."

_____ 50. "Hail King, for so thou art. Behold where stands
Th' usurper's cursed head."

_____ 51. "I go alone, and it is done. The bell invites me.
Hear it not, Duncan, for it is a knell
That summons thee to heaven, or to hell."

_____ 52. "Front to front
Bring thou this fiend of Scotland and myself.
Within my sword's length set him. If he scape,
Heaven forgive him too!"

© Novel Units, Inc.   All rights reserved

Name_____

Macbeth
OBJECTIVE UNIT EXAM
page 8

True-False.

_____ 53. Hecate is not concerned that she was not included in the first meeting with Macbeth.

_____ 54. Lady Macbeth is as strong a character at the end of the play as she was at the start.

_____ 55. Malcolm becomes king at the end of the play just as his father originally intended.

_____ 56. Lady Macbeth's handwashing is a manifestation of her guilt.

_____ 57. "Blood will have blood" means that violence begets more violence.

_____ 58. The news of his family's murder was brought to Macduff by Malcolm.

_____ 59. As a result of his visits to the witches, Macbeth became more and more insecure and worried.

_____ 60. Malcolm misrepresented himself to Macduff because he wanted to play a practical joke on him.

Short Essay. (Use the back of your paper or a separate sheet.)

A. Describe the four apparitions that appeared to Macbeth on his second meeting with the witches, and the warning or meaning of each.

B. What made Macbeth so confident at the end of the play? What was it about Macduff that surprised him and led to his demise?

C. How did Lady Macbeth change from Act I to Act V?

D. Why is the appearance of Banquo's ghost so significant?

Name_____

Macbeth
ESSAY EXAM

Short Essay. Answer ALL of the following. Write one brief but concise paragraph for each.

1. Discuss the following line in relation to the play: "Nothing is but what is not."

2. Agree or disagree and give reasons for your answer:
   a. *Macbeth* is a play about ambition and a lust for power.
   b. *Macbeth* is a play about conscience and insanity.
   c. *Macbeth* is a play about the powers of good and evil.

Longer Essay. Write a three-to-five paragraph essay on both
  (1) the first question below **and**
  (2) your choice of one of the remaining questions.

3. In his struggle to gain and hold the crown of Scotland, Macbeth is driven from one foul deed to another. Discuss the sequence of events from a cause-and-effect standpoint.

4. Discuss the relationship between Lord and Lady Macbeth and its function in the play.

5. Choose one of the following symbols and discuss its use throughout the play: darkness, blood, light, illusion vs. reality.

6. Compare the moral standards of Banquo and Macbeth.

7. Was Macbeth a pawn of Fate or an agent of free will? Be sure to include the role of the witches in your essay.

8. Agree or disagree, and support your answer: In *Macbeth,* Shakespeare was exploring the great capacity for good and evil in the same human heart.

Answer Key

Anticipation Guide: Students' answers will vary. Results should be discussed with the class as a whole group.

Act I Vocabulary: Students should have modern definitions for all words except *heath* Elizabethan meanings: heath: an open place outdoors; broil: battle; posters: swift travelers; fantastical: imaginary; addition: title; missives: messengers; round: crown; illness: ruthlessness; seat: site; convince: overcome.

Act II Vocabulary: Students' rephrasings will vary. Samples: (1) I'll speak with you about it so long as it involves no wrong-doing. (2) The bell reminds me it's time to kill Duncan. I hope it doesn't wake him up. (3) The thing we fear is being caught. Killing Duncan is no problem. (4) I have so much guilt about this that if guilt were blood, the ocean would turn red. (5) Duncan is dead! (6) With Duncan dead, there is little left to make life worth living.

Act III Vocabulary: (1) verities (2) oracles (3) parricide (4) rebuked (5) gospelled (6) avouch (7) scorched (8) jocund (9) vizards (10) measure (11) nonpareil (12) avaunt

Act IV Vocabulary: (1) foisons (2) laudable (3) cauldron (4) adder (5) coz (6) folly (7) brinded (8) gin (9) unsanctified (10) stamp (11) germains (12) birthdom (13) at a point (14) relation (15) slab (16) entrails (17) bodements (18) sceptres (19) blood-boltered (20) pernicious (21) firstlings (22) homely (23) dolor (24) redress (25) affeered (26) impediments (27) portable (28) precise

Act V Vocabulary: <u>Across</u>: 3. guise, 5. kinsmen, 7. patch, 9. sovereign, 11. vulnerable, 13. moe, 14. knolled; <u>Down</u>: 1. ague, 2. gentlewoman, 4. intrenchant, 6. cast, 8. bruited, 10. famine, 12. fell

Study Questions
1. Macbeth
2. He will be executed. Macbeth will receive his title.
3. They hail him as Thane of Glamis, Thane of Cawdor and King hereafter.
4. Macbeth will be Cawdor and King; Banquo will father kings.
5. Banquo is more cautious.
6. trusting, kind
7. Malcolm will be the next king.
8. in a letter from Macbeth

Study Questions, cont.

9. He is too kind to take the easy way to the throne, i.e. murder Duncan.
10. Student answers will vary, but they should note that Lady Macbeth is very cordial to Duncan, yet she plans to kill him.
11. At first he doesn't want to; later he gives in.
12. She asks him if he is a man, calls him a coward.
13. a way to make the predictions come true/ Banquo is willing to discuss it as long as it will require no wrong-doing.
14. a bloody dagger
15. He reminded her of her father. Macbeth killed him.
16. Lady Macbeth is calm and collected, while Macbeth raves that he will never sleep peacefully again and that the oceans will turn red from the blood on his hands.
17. Macduff and Lennox
18. Macduff
19. Macbeth feigns grief and kills the guards. Lady Macbeth faints.
20. Duncan's sons. They go to England and Ireland.
21. Macbeth
22. He is a threat because of the prediction that he will father kings.
23. Banquo is killed but Fleance escapes.
24. Banquo's ghost appears, causing Macbeth to exhibit strange behavior. Lady Macbeth makes excuses for him and asks the guests to leave.
25. Queen of the Witches; Her involvement with Macbeth's fate lets us know this is an important event, not something to be handled by underling witches.
26. England—to meet with Malcolm and King Edward regarding the mustering of forces to oust Macbeth.
27. He is beginning to believe everything they say. Now he wants to know his future.
28. An armed head tells Macbeth to beware of Macduff; a bloody child tells him that no man of woman born shall harm him; a child carrying a branch of a tree tells him he will not be vanquished until Birnam Wood comes to Dunsinane (his castle). The final apparition is of eight kings followed by a smiling Banquo.
29. by killing his wife and children
30. assurance of his patriotism and concern for Scotland
31. He will give them 10,000 soldiers.
32. Lady Macbeth has lost her self-assurance. She now sleepwalks, confessing to the murders, and has developed the habit of compulsively washing her hands. Her conscience has driven her insane, and Macbeth is of no help to her since he has turned into a bloodthirsty madman himself.

33. He is not "a big enough man" to fill Duncan's place.
34. because of the messages of the apparitions
35. They cut branches from Birnam Wood for camouflage as they move toward the castle.
36. She commits suicide.
37. "No man of woman born shall harm Macbeth."
38. He was not "of woman born." His birth was a Caesarean.
39. Macbeth's head
40. Malcolm

Activity #8: Answers will vary.
Activity #9: Answers will vary.
Activity #10: Sociogram: Duncan was very trusting of Macbeth, and thought him a brave soldier. Macbeth liked Duncan, too, but was miffed that he named Malcolm as his successor. He didn't want to kill him, but there seemed to be no choice if he wanted to be king. Lady Macbeth treats Macbeth as something of a child, manipulating him cleverly to do what she wants. Macbeth is apparently putty in her hands. Macbeth and Banquo are good friends at the beginning of the play, but Banquo is rather suspicious of the witches' predictions, while Macbeth believes them. Banquo would not harm Macbeth, but we are not so sure, at this point, what Macbeth might do to Banquo. Macbeth sees Macduff as another nobleman whose support he needs; Macduff, however, is suspicious of what Macbeth is up to.
Activity #11: Students should mark the verse like the example. Their original lines should follow the same pattern.
Activity #12: Students' answers may vary. Some sample answers: Act I, iii—"So foul and fair a day I have not seen." "Lesser than Macbeth, and greater." "Not so happy, yet much happier." "...nothing is but what is not." Act II, i—"I have thee not and yet I see thee still." ii—"The death of each day's life..." iii—"...it makes him, and it mars him; it sets him on, and it takes him off; it persuades him, and disheartens him; makes him stand to, and not stand to." iv—"By th' clock 'tis day, And yet dark night strangles the travelling lamp."
Activity #13: (1) simile; honors and garments (2) metaphor; growing seeds and time passing (3) simile; signs of nobleness and stars (4) metaphor; the owl is a messenger of death, the "fatal bellman" (5) metaphor; sleep is a needle that knits the "raveled sleave of care" (another metaphor here—the "sleave of care"), sleep is like death, like a soothing bath. (6) simile; Macbeth's mental state is compared to marble, rock, and air.
Activity #14: Students' answers will vary. Some possible descriptors of Macbeth at the beginning are: loyal, brave, honorable, kind-hearted, gullible. After Act IV he might be described as tyrannical, crazy, bloodthirsty, carried away by power.
Activity #15: Students' answers will vary somewhat, and should be discussed with a partner and/or the whole class.
Activity #16: Ideally, you will be able to use this activity as an introduction to a class project which can be produced on a desktop-publishing system.

Activity #17: Center circle: Macbeth, Lady Macbeth. **Second circle:** The Witches and Hecate, Duncan, Banquo, Macduff, Malcolm, Ross, Lennox, three murderers
Third circle: Donalbain, Menteith, Angus, Caithness, Fleance, Siward, Young Siward, Seyton, Macduff's wife, Macduff's son, a captain, two doctors, a porter, an old man, a gentlewoman, a lord **Fourth circle:** various lords, officers, soldiers, messengers, attendants. Passers-by in the scene with the old man outside the castle.
Activity #18: Lists of various groups will vary depending on the act they are assigned.
Activity #19: Use for review after reading; cooperative activity. Discuss answers in class for further review.

Vocabulary Quiz
1. B
2. A
3. C
4. B
5. B
6. C
7. B
8. B
9. C
10. B
11. B
12. A
13. C
14. I
15. M
16. C
17. L
18. D
19. E
20. B
21. F
22. A
23. G
24. K
25. J
26. H
27. E
28. L
29. M
30. B
31. I
32. N
33. A
34. K
35. G
36. F
37. J
38. C
39. H
40. D

Act One Quiz
1. B
2. D
3. D
4. D
5. C
6. A
7. D
8. C
9. B
10. C

Act Two Quiz
1. C
2. B
3. B
4. D
5. C
6. D
7. C
8. D
9. C
10. A

Act Three Quiz
1. C
2. A
3. F
4. C
5. B
6. D
7. E
8. B
9. A
10. G
11. T
12. F
13. F
14. F
15. F
16. T
17. T
18. T
19. T
20. T

Act Four Quiz
1. the witches
2. an armed head: "Beware Macduff."
3. a bloody child: "No man of woman born shall harm Macbeth."
4. a child holding a branch: "Macbeth shall not be vanquished until great Birnam Wood comes to high Dunsinane Hill."
5. eight kings followed by Banquo—Macbeth is enraged.

© Novel Units, Inc. All rights reserved

Act Four Quiz, continued

6. with Malcolm in England
7. Macduff's wife and children
8. He was testing Macduff's patriotism.
9. Ross
10. He will kill Macbeth.

Objective Unit Exam

1.	B	11.	B	21.	D	31.	B	41.	B	51. C
2.	B	12.	A	22.	A	32.	B	42.	F	52. E
3.	A	13.	D	23.	C	33.	C	43.	C	53. F
4.	D	14.	D	24.	E	34.	B	44.	G	54. F
5.	C	15.	A	25.	B	35.	A	45.	A	55. T
6.	C	16.	B	26.	C	36.	E	46.	D	56. T
7.	B	17.	E	27.	B	37.	B	47.	B	57. T
8.	A	18.	A	28.	A	38.	A	48.	F	58. F
9.	C	19.	C	29.	A	39.	D	49.	A	59. F
10.	E	20.	D	30.	B	40.	E	50.	G	60. F

Short Essay

A. See answers to Study Questions, #28.
B. He had put his faith totally in the apparitions' messages and believed his life was "charmed." When Macduff revealed he was born by Caesarean, not "of woman," the end was inevitable.
C. She was self-assured, confident, and practical at the beginning, albeit rather ruthless and power-hungry. By the end, her guilt had driven her insane.
D. It is the turning point of the play. After this, Macbeth begins to behave very irrationally. His life begins a downward spiral.